Willie M:

Secrets of Pets: Care of Fishes.

ISBN-13: 978-1721875368

ISBN-10: 1721875360

TABLE OF CONTENTS

HOW TO CHOOSE A FISH? 5
    DANIOS: 6
    GLOFISH: 7
    ANGELFISH: 8
    KUHLI LOACH: 9
    GUPPIES: 10
    BLACK MOLLY: 11
    CICHLIDS: 12
    OTOCINCLUS CATFISH: 13
    JACK DEMPSEY: 15
    AROWANA: 16
    THE GREEN SWORDTAIL: 17
    WHITE CLOUD MOUNTAIN MINNOWS: 19
    GOLDFISH: 20
    TETRA: 21
    POINTS TO REMEMBER BEFORE BUYING FISH FOR YOUR AQUARIUM: 23
    WHICH FISH ARE THE RIGHT CHOICE FOR YOUR AQUARIUM? 24
    RECOMMENDATIONS ON HOW TO CHOOSE AND COMBINE THE SELECTED FISH IN THE AQUARIUM: 24
    POINTS TO REMEMBER WHILE CHOOSING FISH AS A BEGINNER: 26

HOW TO CHOOSE AN AQUARIUM? 27
    DESCRIPTION OF VARIETIES OF AQUARIUMS: 27
    FRESHWATER TROPICAL AQUARIUM: 27
    COLD WATER AQUARIUMS: 28
    MARINE AQUARIUMS: 29
    BRACKISH AQUARIUMS: 30
    RECOMMENDATIONS FOR CHOOSING AN AQUARIUM: 30
    SIZE OF THE AQUARIUM: 31
    AQUARIUM MADE UP OF ACRYLIC OR GLASS: 31
    CHOOSING EQUIPMENTS FOR YOUR AQUARIUM FROM BUDGET TO LUXURY KIT: 32
    HEATERS FOR FRESHWATER TROPICAL AQUARIUM: 33
    USE OF THERMOMETERS: 34
    FILTERS FOR YOUR AQUARIUM: 35
    PLANTS FOR AQUARIUM: 36
    GRAVEL SUBSTRATE FOR AQUARIUMS: 37
    A CANOPY OR A HOOD: 38
    STAND OR CABINET FOR THE AQUARIUM: 39
    POWER HEADS: 39

AIR PUMP FOR THE AQUARIUM: 40
PROPER LIGHTING: 41
MISCELLANEOUS CLEANING TOOLS 41
BUCKET FOR WATER CHANGES 42
NETS 42
RECOMMENDATIONS FOR BUYING AFFORDABLE EQUIPMENTS: 42
OPT FOR THE USED AQUARIUM: 43
BUYING FISH FROM OTHER AQUARIUM OWNERS: 43
SPEND LESS ON ELECTRICITY BILLS: 43
USE HIGH QUALITY ACCESSORIES: 44
MAKE USE OF LED LIGHTS: 44
SPENDING LESS AMOUNT ON PLANTS: 44
GETTING THE BROKEN EQUIPMENT REPAIRED: 45
RECOMMENDATIONS ON HOW TO MAKE AN AQUARIUM WITH YOUR OWN HANDS: 45
SELECTION AND PREPARATION OF THE GLASS: 45
OTHER ESSENTIAL ITEMS: 46
HOW AND WHERE TO INSTALL THE AQUARIUM: 48
STRENGTH OF THE FLOOR TO RETAIN WEIGHT: 48
DISTANCE OF THE ELECTRICAL OUTLET FROM ACQUARIUM: 48
WATER SUPPLY HAS TO BE AT HAND: 48

CREATING A COMFORTABLE LIVING ENVIRONMENT 49

RECOMMENDATIONS FOR FILLING THE AQUARIUM (SOIL, ALGAE, DECOR ELEMENTS, LIGHTING EQUIPMENT): 49
LOCATION OF THE AQUARIUM: 49
THE PROCESS OF FILLING THE GRAVEL: 50
LAYING THE SUBSTRATE IN AQUARIUM: 51
HEATERS AND LIGHTS FOR AQUARIUM: 51
CLEANING THE FILTERS: 52
DECORATIVE ELEMENTS: 52
DESCRIPTION OF HOW TO CONTROL WATER PARAMETERS AT INITIAL STAGES: 53
pH CONTENT IN AQUARIUM WATER: 53
THERMOMETER: 54
PROPER AERATION: 55
AIR PUMPS FOR AQUARIUM: 55
AQUARIUM AIR STONES: 55
AIR HOSE: 55
FILTERING THE AQUARIUM WATER: 55
INTERNAL BOX FILTER: 57
EXTERNAL POWER FILTER: 57
EXTERNAL CANISTER FILTER: 58

UNDER GRAVEL FILTER: 58
THE NITROGEN CYCLE: 59
THE PROCESS OF LAUNCHING FISH INTO THE AQUARIUM: 59

PROPER CARE FOR FISH 61

ESSENTIAL VITAMINS FOR YOUR FISH: 62
RECOMMENDATIONS FOR MONITORING THE LIFE OF AQUARIUM: 63
CLEANLINESS OF THE AQUARIUM: 63
MAINTENANCE OF THE FILTERS: 64
CONTROLLING ALGAE: 64
TEST THE WATER OF AQUARIUM FROM TIME TO TIME: 66
PARTIAL REPLACEMENT OF WATER: 66
RECOMMENDATIONS FOR MONITORING THE LIFE OF FISH AND FEEDING THEM : 67
HOW TO FEED THE FISH IN YOUR AQUARIUM: 69
MAINTENANCE OF THE AQUARIUM: 71
TASKS TO BE PERFORMED WEEKLY: 71
WORKS TO BE DONE AFTER A MONTH: 72
TASKS TO BE DONE ON QUARTERLY BASIS: 72
MAINTENANCE OF AQUARIUM AFTER A YEAR: 72
HEALTH OF THE FISH IN AQUARIUM: 73
DESCRIPTION OF SYMPTOMS AND DISEASES OF THE FISH AND CURES: 73
COMMON AILMENTS AFFECTING FISH: 74
RECOMMENDATIONS ON DRUGS AND TREATMENT: 77
MEASURES FOR DISEASE PREVENTION: 78

How to Choose a Fish?

If you are eager about having a freshwater aquarium at home or workplace, first you need to be well acquainted with different fish species that get along with one another and can coexist. You cannot merely start filling your aquarium with fish hastily. You must be conversant with terms like coldwater aquarium, tropical aquarium, community aquarium etc. You too need to have a proper knowledge of different fish species, the water temperature they need to survive, their growth rate, temperament, etc. Once you become well versed with the requirements of fish rearing, you can go ahead with having the aquarium of your choice.

We are going to facilitate the task of choosing the right fish species for you. Let us enumerate the famous fish breeds that can be the proper choice for the aquarium of your dream.

Let us start with the popular fish species suitable for heated freshwater aquariums.

Danios:

One of the most popular freshwater aquarium fish are Danios. Perfect for community aquarium, this fish species is known for its active and agile temperament. Due to their ability to survive in difficult conditions, they are perfect for those who are beginners in rearing fish. They can not only survive in different water conditions and temperatures but are also quite active and lively. As they are omnivorous, they accept a wide variety of food and do very well with flakes. If you are planning to start with fish rearing, Danios can be the most suitable option for you. Most of the species belonging to Danios family are bright colored. About 3" inch in size, they need the minimum water tank size of 10 gallons.

GloFish

A type of Danio fish, GloFish are best known for their shimmering and glowing ability. Peaceful in temperament, the GloFish have best surviving rates if they are kept with other peaceful species. Their fluorescent body makes them glow in dark and children love watching the glowing movements in the water tanks. They best survive in water temperature ranging between 65 to 75 degree Fahrenheit. Approximately 2 to 2.5 inches in size, these fish need to be fed on an omnivorous diet.

Angelfish:

Another popular species is the angelfish that is rather tall. About 6 inches in size, this fish is peaceful in temperament. These need to be kept with other peaceful species as aggressive fish species tend to make them nervous. They survive best in the water temperature ranging from 75 to 82 degree Fahrenheit. You need to have a well established aquarium with stable water conditions as the fluctuations in temperature tend to make them nervous and stressed. They require dense plants where they stay peacefully and quietly. They do well with other peaceful fish species like black mollies and neon tetra. They eat smaller fish. Their beautiful and colorful appearance attract people.

Kuhli Loach:

An eel-like fish, the Kuhli Loach is another popular fish species. Their ability to keep the tank clean by eating the food that lies at the bottom makes them a popular choice for aquarists. A unique bottom dweller, it loves to hide in gravel or sand lying at the bottom of aquarium. They are good at keeping the aquarium clean as they eat the food fallen at the bottom of the tank. It can live up to 10 years and grows up to 10 cm in length. They need the minimum water tank size of 15 gallons with the water temperature ranging between 75 and 86 degree Fahrenheit. Kuhli Loach thrives best in an aquarium if kept with 5 or 6 fish of its kind.

Guppies:

Another peaceful breed of fish that is easy to take care for is Guppy. It is loved by beginners as it is a very hardy fish. If kept with other fish species, they have less surviving rates. They can be fed on an omnivorous diet. A female guppy can give birth to 60 babies at the most. The female is usually bigger and more hardy with a rather small tail. The male guppy is more colorful with a larger tail. It survives best in a temperature ranging between 64 to 82 degree Fahrenheit in the minimum tank size of 20 gallons. Their average size is 2 to 3" inches and prefer small groups of 4 to 6 fish.

Black Molly:

Black Molly is a perfect option for beginners because of their hardiness and a wide range of colors and varieties. They are good at surviving in different water conditions. They have the unique ability to survive in brackish, fresh or salt water. The mollies need the minimum water tank size of 30 gallons with a number of tough plants as this fish breed has the tendency to destroy the softer plants. They have the ability to survive in different water temperatures ranging from 70 to 82 degree Fahrenheit. As this fish species is omnivorous, it can be fed upon any kind of food such as flakes, plants and worms. Peaceful in nature, they should not be kept with aggressive fish species.

Cichlids:

Cichlids are a famous fish breed. They can grow up to 8" length if given proper care and food. The suitable tank size for this species is around 70 gallons and the suitable water temperature for them is between 76 to 82 degrees Fahrenheit. The electric blue cichlid is one of the best known and aggressive variants of Cichlids.

Otocinclus Catfish:

If you are a beginner in the fish rearing, the Otocinclus Catfish can be an appropriate option for you. This fish breed is affordable, hardy and easy to maintain. Quite peaceful in temperament, this fish should be kept in the tank size of at least 30 gallons. As they are not as colourful and attractive as many other fish breeds, they are generally overlooked. They survive best in the water temperature ranging between 74 to 79 degrees Fahrenheit.

The Glass Catfish:

This fish species is one of the few aquarium Catfish that does not stay at the bottom of the aquarium. They are mid-water fish and thrive in the mid section of the aquarium. Approximately 4 inch in size, this fish does best in water temperature ranging 72 to 79 degree Fahrenheit. Like other mid-water fish species, they should be kept with at least four or five of its types. The Glass Catfish has a transparent body. and looks attractive. This is a hardy fish though sometimes it finds it difficult to acclimatize to the aquarium. If you are planning to have a community aquarium, this fish species can be a valuable addition to your collection of fish.

Jack Dempsey:

Another beautiful and colourful fish species is Jack Dempsey. As this fish breed is a hiding species, they should be provided with a bottom filled with plenty of rocks and sand. An aggressive fish breed, Jack Dempsey should not be placed with peaceful fish species. With an average size of around 8 to 10", they must have similar sized fish breeds for companions in the water tank of about 500 gallons. A carnivorous breed, this fish feeds on smaller fish and nutritious food.

Arowana:

Arowana is a popular fish species that is considered unsuitable for aquariums maintained by beginners as these fish are as large as 47 inches. Due to their monstrous size, they are not easy to maintain. It is also called dragonfish due to its resemblance to the Chinese dragon. Suitable for professional aquarists, this fish needs to be kept in large and well filtered aquariums. They survive best in water temperature ranging from 75 to 82 degree Fahrenheit.

The Green Swordtail:

The Green Swordtail is another famous fish species as it breeds fast even when in captivity. The males have a long swordlike growth on the lower part of their tail fin that grows in size as the fish matures. It is recommended to have more females in an aquarium than males as the males are quarrelsome by nature. They harass females can be temperamental and will harass the females. These fish breed every month at 74 degrees Fahrenheit. A major benefit of owning this species is that it prevents the growth of algae.

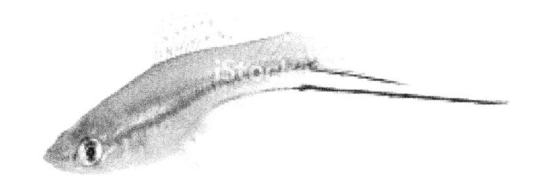

Platy: The Platy closely resembles the Swordtail and they are both very close relatives. It is believed by many to be the ideal community fish. Many color varieties are available to be reared at home aquarium. Good number of fish in dense vegetation will lead to successful breeding. The Platies are good at consuming algae and survive best when kept in the group of five to seven fish. The ideal temperature for them is 72 to 79 degree Fahrenheit. Being omnivorous, they eat a variety of food. Their normal size is 4 to 4.5 inch.

Let us now enlist the fish species that are suitable for coldwater aquarium:

White Cloud Mountain Minnows:

The white cloud is another small fish that has the ability to survive in cold temperatures even as low as 60 degree Fahrenheit. They live in a community and can survive up to 5 years if given proper care and nutritious food. Peaceful in temperament, they are suitable for community aquarium as they get along with other peaceful fish species. They tend to live at the top or middle of the water tank and rarely go down to the bottom of the aquarium.

Goldfish:

Another major species of hardy fish is Goldfish that come in different colours and sizes. They are loved by people for their beauty and eye-catching appearance. If you are a beginner, goldfish is an ideal option for you as it is quite easy to keep them. This fish species survive best in water temperature ranging between 62 and 74 degree Fahrenheit. You must replace almost 10% of the water from aquarium every week for good results. These fish are good at adapting themselves to diverse aquarium conditions. They are also not choosy about food and readily eat whatever is offered to them.

Tetra:

One of the most popular freshwater tropical fish for aquarium is tetra. This fish comes in a wide variety of colours and species. An easy to keep fish species, tetras are loved for their hardiness. The neon tetra is one of the most famous species of tetra. An omnivorous fish species, tetras can be fed upon both plants and worms. Tetras are quite small and prone to be eaten by bigger fish. They prefer to live in groups and in an aquarium, there must be at least 6 to 7 tetras living together. Their size varies from 0.25 to 1.25" inches with the average life span of 2 to 5 years.

Criteria for Selecting the Desired Fish (requirement for water temperature, size, level of aggression, requirement for water quality, price):

The task of selecting the fish species for your aquarium is not an easy one. There are so many fish species in the market that one can easily get confused about the what species to choose and what to reject. You must be well acquainted with the characteristics, temperaments and varieties of the fish before you select the fish for your water tank. The aquarium must be ready before buying fish so that when the fish are brought home, they are at once placed in the aquarium.

You must keep in mind the living conditions of the different fish species. Some fish are quite hardy and have better surviving rates. Some are so tender and weak that a minor change in the temperature of the water may prove fatal to them.

If you want to set up cold water tank, fish breeds compatible with cold water will be suitable for your aquarium. the tropical fish species will be appropriate for your aquarium if you have warm water. You may have to install a heater to keep the water at the desired temperature for the tropical fish.

You must also keep in mind the compatibility of different fish breeds if you are planning to put together different species.

It is easier to manage a fresh water tank than a marine or salt water tank. Guppies, Angel fish, Gold fish , Mollies, White Cloud Mountain fish are some of the best known fresh water fish species. They are most suitable for beginners as they have better surviving rates and can live at room temperatures.

The tropical fish species are colourful, attractive and ornamental. Clown fish and damsel fish are some of the most suitable options for beginners. Lionfish and Dragonets are suitable for experienced fish breeders.

Points to remember before buying fish for your Aquarium:

After you have made the decision about the variety of fish species for your aquarium, you must go in for the reliable and trustworthy seller of fish. A seller who has a good reputation of selling healthy and affordable fish breeds should be preferred by you. Make sure that the fish you have bought is healthy. Avoid buying fish with sores on their body. Avoid buying such fish as appear sluggish, diseased and nervous. You must prefer active, agile and alert fish.

Also keep in mind the different breeds that go well together and avoid buying such species as are not compatible with one another. Do keep in mind size of the fish breeds. Even after putting the fish in aquarium, keep an eye on their movements and see how they get along with one another. If you find any fish afflicted with a disease, make arrangements to separate it from others.

Which Fish Are the Right Choice for Your Aquarium?

While maintaining an aquarium, you need to keep in mind a few points. You must consider the temperament of the fish species that you want to rear.

You can choose different fish breeds to populate your aquarium. But you must keep in mind the temperament of the different fish breeds so that they don't harm one another and coexist peacefully. An aquarium filled with varied breeds and different coloured fishes look attractive.

The size of the fish also matters a lot. Small sized fish shouldn't be accommodated with large fish breeds as the big fish can suffocate small fish species.

Recommendations on how to choose and combine the selected fish in the aquarium:

Before buying the fish breed of your choice, you must acquaint yourself fully with the suitable living conditions all the fish breed you are planning to own. You can get the necessary information from a library, internet or from someone who is an expert in this field.

Fish breeds can be categorized into freshwater and saltwater fish. They can further be subdivided into cold water and tropical fish species. If freshwater fish breeds are easier to look after, salt water fish breeding is suitable for experienced aquarists. Coldwater fish species survive best in water temperature ranging between 18 and 22 degrees Celsius whereas the tropical fish species require water temperature ranging from 24 to 30 degree Celsius. You can install a heater for the grooming of tropical fish breeds in the best suitable conditions.

Having finalized the fish species for your aquarium, you must consider the compatibility of the different fish breeds that you are going to house together. Peaceful fish species must be placed with similar docile and peace-loving fish species. Never combine aggressive fish breeds with those that are peaceful and docile. Mixing different species together is an important task and needs to be done with a lot of care and precision.

It is also very important to keep in mind the size of the fully grown fish that you intend to keep in your aquarium. Be very particular about the size of the fish species as there are some fish breeds that grow very fast and become too large. Whereas there are some fish species that do not grow fast enough to be accommodated with other fast growing fish species.

Once you have decided about the fish species, water quality and temperature etc., you can go ahead with the task of adding fish to your carefully established aquarium. While putting fish into the aquarium, avoid overcrowding the water tank and also avoid putting wrong fish together.

It is best to begin with two or three hardy fish and observe them for the first ten days. Thereafter add two or three more to the aquarium and again observe them for another ten days. If you put too many fish into a new aquarium at once, the water will not cycle adequately and will quickly turn toxic. You have to be quite patient for the first 6-8 weeks. Once the nitrogen cycle is complete, you can add additional fish. You need to exercise moderation while adding fish to the aquarium.

As a beginner, you must minutely observe the behaviour of the fish and consult an expert in this field to avoid all possible difficulties.

Points to remember while choosing fish as a beginner:

One might be fascinated by the beautiful colors and captivating looks of the fish but there are other important factors to consider before you go in for the selection of fish. You must give preference to the fish species with the following qualities:

The fish must be omnivorous so that they accept a wide variety of foods.

They must survive in different water conditions.

Peaceful fish species must be preferred to aggressive ones.

The compatibility with other fish breeds is another major requirement.

Start by adding 2 or 3 fish in a new aquarium and gradually add 2 or 3 more as the water tank becomes cycled.

How to Choose an Aquarium?

Description of Varieties of Aquariums:

Freshwater aquariums are the most common water tanks for fish lovers. If you are a novice in fish rearing, you must start with freshwater aquariums. They are easy to maintain, affordable and house a wide variety of fish species. Freshwater aquariums can further be divided into freshwater tropical aquariums and freshwater cold water aquariums.

Freshwater Tropical Aquarium:

It is quite easy to keep the freshwater tropical aquariums and that is why they are ideal for beginners in owning aquariums. The ideal water temperature of tropical aquariums ranges between 72 and 84 Degrees Fahrenheit. Tropical fish species are quite affordable and are not as expensive as the marine fish breeds. There is a wide variety of fish species that can adapt to the freshwater tropical aquariums. Before going in for the marine water aquariums, you must have an experience of having freshwater tropical water tanks.

Cold Water Aquariums:

Cold water aquariums too are a good option to start with the hobby of owning an aquarium. The water temperature is kept beneath 70 degrees or rather at room temperature. There are a number of fish species that get along the cold water aquariums. Goldfish is the most common of these species. One of the most common cold water species kept in a cold water aquarium is the Goldfish. Many people had goldfish bowls as a children. Lots of people today own Goldfish Aquariums. Cold water freshwater fish may be a bit more expensive than the standard goldfish. Koi and goldfish ponds are great examples of domesticated cold water fish habitats.

Marine Aquariums:

Marine aquariums are filled with salt water for some particular fish species to survive. You must buy salt and mix it with water to be put in the water tank. These aquariums can either be filled with natural seawater or supplied with water mixed with artificial salts purchased from shops. It is more difficult to maintain a marine aquarium than a freshwater aquarium. One has to have a long experience of owning freshwater aquarium before one shifts to saltwater aquarium. The saltwater fish species are also more expensive than freshwater fish breeds and require a lot more effort and care on one's part to maintain marine water tank.

Brackish Aquariums:

The third but rare variety of aquariums is brackish water aquariums. Brackish water is a mix of freshwater and saltwater. It stands somewhere between the two with less salinity than the marine water and saltier than freshwater.

The selection of fish is quite difficult with very few suitable for such water conditions. The Puffer also known as the Freshwater Puffer is actually a brackish water fish. It is even more difficult to maintain brackish water aquariums than marine water aquariums due to rare water conditions.

Recommendations for choosing an aquarium:

It is not an easy task to select the right aquarium for your fish. You need to take into account a number of factors before finalizing the water tank for your home or workplace. The aquarium must get along the place at which you install it and it must also be big enough to accommodate the size and number of fish. We have taken it upon ourselves to facilitate the task of choosing the right aquarium for all your requirements.

Size of the Aquarium:

The first thing you must keep in mind is the size of the aquarium. The tank should be big enough to accommodate the fish species you are going to put in it. You can go in for the big size as it will provide enough space for the fish to move in it. The greater the volume of water, the less will be the toxins in aquarium. You must also keep in mind your budget before you finalize the aquarium.

Aquarium made up of Acrylic or Glass:

The next important point that must be considered before buying is the make of the aquarium. You can choose a glass aquarium or an acrylic made aquarium. You must know the pros and cons of both these materials before you go in for the suitable aquarium. Glass aquariums are usually not as expensive as acrylic aquariums. They are also more scratch resistant. Acrylic aquariums, on the other hand, are sturdier and stiffer than glass though they are less scratch resistant. The acrylic aquariums are light weight and easier to carry. It is also easier to repair acrylic than glass. You can also make the decision about the make of the aquarium as per your liking and taste.

Choosing Equipments for your Aquarium from Budget to Luxury Kit:

After you have chosen the suitable aquarium for fish keeping, you need to select the appropriate accessories and equipments that perfectly match your aquarium and get along with it. There are a number of accessories available in the market and you may get confused by the bewildering variety of each equipment. Some are essential, some are useless. You must be able to differentiate between what is required and what is to be avoided. You can consult some professional aquarist and buy what is perfect for all your needs.

Let us get started with the types of aquariums. There are only two types i.e. acrylic and glass. Both have their own pros and cons. Glass aquariums are usually cheaper than acrylic aquariums. Good quality glasses are scratch resistant but ordinary glasses are prone to scratches. Acrylic aquariums too get scratches easily but they can be fixed. Glass aquariums weigh more than acrylic aquariums even when empty. Glass aquariums can break easily, whereas acrylic tanks are harder to break.

Usually people prefer glass acquariums. You can choose the one that is in accordance with your needs and budget.

When it comes to the size of the aquarium, you'd better choose large aquarium rather than smaller one. Large aquariums provide more space for fish to move about. If there is any contamination in water, it spreads faster in small aquarium than large water tanks. Maintenance of both the large and small aquariums is almost same. Large aquariums also look more beautiful.

A larger aquarium can house more fish. Instead of increasing the volume of water, more surface area will be a better option as many fish species tend to spend their whole lives near bottom. There are also too many fish breeds that move about at the middle and many dwell on the top.

As a beginner in aquarium keeping, you can start with 20 to 25 gallon aquarium and as you become more experienced, you can shift towards owning bigger aquariums. Too small aquariums should not be preferred as they don't allow enough space for fish to swim.

Heaters for Freshwater Tropical Aquarium:

If you intend to have a freshwater tropical aquarium, a heater is a must. It helps the water stay warm without letting it go cold. For the tropical fish species, the ideal water temperature ranges between 74 to 84 degree Fahrenheit. A good quality heater maintains the water temperature at the required level for tropical fish aquarium. Water heaters mainly come in two types i.e. submersible heaters and partially submersible heaters.

Submersible heaters remain immersed in water as they are installed at the bottom of aquarium. Usually these heaters are fixed horizontally at the bottom of the aquarium. These heaters are in trend nowadays as they not only maintain the temperature inside the aquarium but also remain secure when water is changed.

The partially immersed water heaters are traditional and come in the form of a glass tube with heating coils. One has to be quite careful while using these water heaters. When water is being changed, this traditional heater needs to be unplugged or else the tube may get damaged.

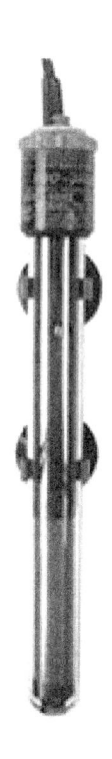

Use of Thermometers:

Thermometers are needed to make sure that water inside the aquarium stays uniform and at the required temperature. The traditional thermometers work just like the ones we normally use at home. They are kept at the surface of water and you can constantly monitor the temperature of water in aquarium. While buying a thermometer, go in for the good quality thermometer that shows right readings.

Filters for your Aquarium:

Aquariums generally have three types of filters i.e. biological, chemical and mechanical. Biological filter is a must for every aquarium as this system of filtration is not only cheap but also most effective in decomposing toxic ammonia.

Chemical filter makes use of chemical such as zeolite and activated carbon to get rid of toxic ammonia, dissolved impurities and other harmful metals.

Mechanical filter removes such substances as particles of food, leaves, remnants of plants before they become toxic.

High quality filter systems consists of all the above three filtering processes. Mechanical filter is also called pre-filter that removes particles of food, plants and leaves. Chemical filter is optional as it is a short-term requirement only. Both biological and mechanical filters needs maintenance from time to time as they may get clogged due to the accumulation of debris.

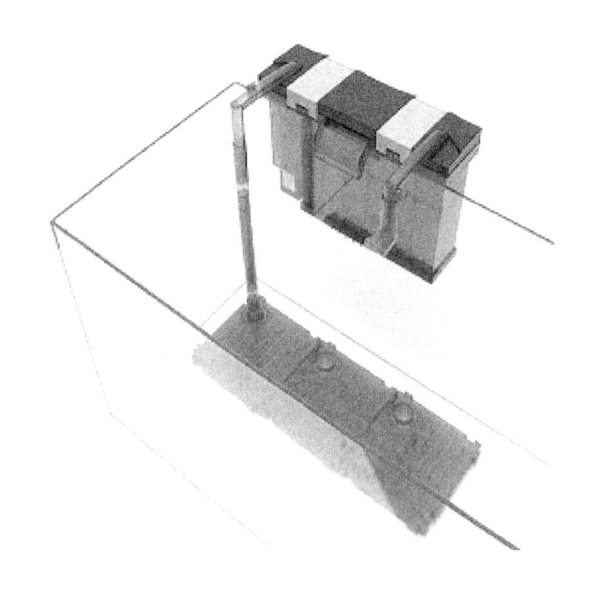

Plants for Aquarium:

Plants serve two basic purposes. They provide hiding places for fish and decorate the aquarium. There are real and plastic plants for aquarium. Real plants need to be taken care of and plastic plants are easier to maintain. If you want to have real plants in your aquarium, you'd better consult a professional aquarist for all the requirements.

Gravel Substrate for Aquariums:

There must be right gravel substrate for the desired growth of real plants. Gravel provides hiding places for fish species that lie at bottom. the ideal gravel size is 2 to 3 mm. Larger pieces of gravel can hurt fish and can also keep food from the reach of fish. These food particles subsequently affect the quality of the water and may cause serious diseases to the fish. Natural gravel is preferred to bright substrate as too bright colours may make fish nervous and uncomfortable.

Wash the gravel properly with warm or lukewarm water so that its impurities get eliminated.To start with, spread a layer of fertilizer and add another gravel layer of about 2 cm on it. Hereafter make a smooth surface with one more layer of gravel. The substrate has to be 3 to 6 cm thick.

A Canopy or a Hood:

A canopy is useful in preventing water for evaporating. Water evaporation at a fast pace may damage heaters and filters. It not only reduces the volume of water but also increases the level of minerals, solvents and other unwanted carbonates in the water tank. A canopy or a hood not only prevents fish from jumping out of the aquarium but also stops contaminants from entering the aquarium. It also helps in maintaining the right temperature.

Stand or Cabinet for the Aquarium:

A proper stand or cabinet is a must for your aquarium. You can buy a proper and suitable stand from the market. The stand has to be smooth and even so that the aquarium is firmly planted on it. It should also be strong enough to withstand the weight of the aquarium filled with water and fish. Uneven stand can break the glass. You can place a 1/4 inch thick sheet of styrofoam on the stand to make aquarium stiffly planted on it. The stand too is to be kept at the place which is also firm and smooth.

Power heads:

A power head is a water pump for aquarium. It remains completely immersed in the water tank. It is used to create flow of water throughout the aquarium. It is also used for the functioning of under gravel filter. Power heads are used to mix together the newly introduced water and old water in the tank. They can also be adjusted to increase oxygenation in water. They are quite affordable and useful in maintaining the required oxygen level in aquarium.

Air Pump for the Aquarium:

Air pumps serve two important purposes. They are used to ensure that your aquarium has an adequate level of oxygen. Secondly, air pumps are used to push water through a filter. In larger tanks, power heads perform the similar function. You need to install an air pump only if your aquarium does not have proper water circulation.

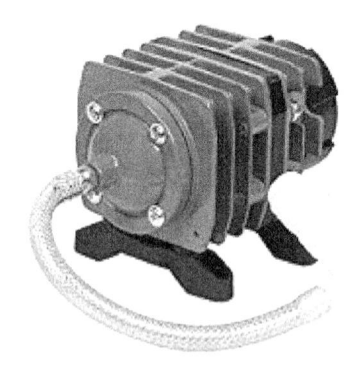

Proper Lighting:

Proper lighting is very important as it highlights the beauty of your aquarium and movement of the fish inside. It also serves the purpose of providing the much needed energy to real plants in the aquarium. You need to keep in mind that if you have no real plants in the tank low-wattage fluorescent bulb will do but if you have real plants inside you need to have more light. Avoid bright lights as they make the fish nervous. Fluorescent bulbs are preferred to incandescent bulbs. Do keep in mind that light promotes the excessive growth of algae.

Miscellaneous Cleaning Tools

Hose or siphon is used to remove water from the tank. The hose has to be clean when you are using it for putting water in the aquarium. Many pipes are available with local aquarists.

When removing water by means of hose, you should vacuum the gravel in the aquarium. Many water changing flexible pipes attached with gravel cleaning device are available in the market. These devices come in the form of a tube that is connected to the siphon and you can stir the gravel with the tube like structure. This process is followed to remove toxic detritus and other unwanted particles from gravel.

You should have a scraper to remove algae from the walls inside the aquarium. Visit the local fish store and buy a scraper with a long handle that enables you to reach the farthest corners.

Bucket For Water Changes

You need to have at least one bucket for removing and pouring water into the aquarium. The bucket meant for putting water into aquarium should not be used for other purposes. Also avoid adding chemicals to the bucket.

Nets

You need to have fish nets too for the purpose of catching fish. You must keep in mind the size of the fish before buying the nets for fish. Always opt for the good quality nets as common nets tend to scrape the skin of fish. Instead of nets, you can use glass jars or plastic bags for carrying fish.

Recommendations for buying Affordable Equipments:

It is generally believed that owning an aquarium is quite expensive. Considering the number of equipments you need to ensure the well being of your fish, having an aquarium is going to burn a hole in your pocket. It is equally expensive to maintain the aquarium. Still there are a number of ways to cut down your expenditure.

Let us take the most effective ways to have budget aquarium at home:

Opt for the Used Aquarium:

If you are going to buy a brand new aquarium from an aquarium dealer, you may have to pay a lot of money but if go in for a used or second-hand aquarium, you will have to pay much less amount. There are so many online sites that sell used aquariums. Some shops sell them at cheap rates.

Before buying the used aquarium, you must make sure that it is not damaged and is in good condition. You must check it thoroughly and buy it only after you are certain of its durability. You can also get it along with accessories like a heater, air pump, filter, artificial plants etc. for quite reasonable price.

Buying Fish from Other Aquarium Owners:

You can also get different varieties of fish at quite an attractive price from other fish keepers. Buying fish from aquarium retailers is going to be an expensive affair whereas purchasing or adopting fish from amateur aquarists is very easy. As reselling fish is quite difficult, they are usually offered free of cost. You may find people who want to give a new home to their fish. It will save you a lot of money if you adopt fish from other aquarium keepers.

Spend Less on Electricity Bills:

Installing a heater is an essential requirement for aquarium keeping. Freshwater tropical aquarium requires uniform water temperature of the warm water. Even if you have a subtropical aquarium, you need to have a heater to prevent fluctuations in water temperature.

As the aquarium heaters use a lot of energy, you can keep your electricity bill low by sticking to lower water temperature. You can save money by choosing fish that do well in a slightly lower temperature of around 74 degree Fahrenheit rather than owning fish that does well at about 79 degree Fahrenheit. Lower temperature means saving energy and money as well.

Use high quality Accessories:

You must also keep in mind that sometimes buying a high quality product at a high price can be cheaper in the long run. If you buy a quality filter, aquarium, heater and gravel, you can save a lot of money in the long run. It is quite frustrating if your filter or heater keeps breaking down repeatedly. Repairing an equipment may cost you a lot and it will also disturb the balance of the aquarium. You must go in for the best quality equipments in the beginning so that you be happy later on.

Make Use of LED Lights:

LED lights are quite expensive initially but you can save a lot of money once you have installed them. They are energy efficient and have longer lives. Less power means less electricity bill. As aquariums use a lot of power, use of LED lights will definitely keep your expenditure under control.

Spending Less Amount on Plants:

Plants not only beauty aquariums but are also essential for the well being of many fish species. It is also to be acknowledged that a well planted aquarium requires a lot of expenditure. If you buy plants from professional aquarium shops, you will have to spend a lot of money.

There are so many places like aquarium forums and groups where you can get cheap plants. Aquarium keepers here usually give away plants for low rates. There are also many varieties of real pants that are quite affordable and easy to maintain.

Getting the Broken Equipment Repaired:

One of the best ways to save money on aquarium keeping is by getting repaired the equipments and accessories of your aquarium. Sometimes having an equipment repaired is going to save you from unnecessary expenditure. There are many people who just dispose off the equipments without thinking that they can be easily repaired. Sometimes, people throw away their tanks if there is a leakage in the aquarium. The leakage can be stopped by merely applying the silicone sealant.

Recommendations on how to make an aquarium with your own hands:

Making an aquarium with your own hands seem to be a daunting task but the fact is it is quite interesting. It will not only save your hard earned money but also provide you the unique learning experience which will further improve your skills of aquarium keeping. You need to have a few essential tools, a big sheet of glass or acrylic. You can design your aquarium as per your own ideas.

Selection and Preparation of the Glass:

One of the most important task to do is to select the right glass or plastic sheet. If you want a glass aquarium, 'sheet glass' also known as 'annealed glass' can be the suitable option for you. It is sturdy and strong enough for the purpose of aquarium. You'd better avoid tempered glass as it does not have enough strength.

If you want a plastic aquarium, polycarbonate plastic can be appropriate for you. Be particular about the proper cutting of glass. Have its edges properly ground so that it doesn't hurt anyone.

Now you have to make a decision about the thickness of the glass sheet. The general rule is to have thick glass so that it doesn't get broken by chance. However you can keep in mind the following criteria while deciding the thickness of the glass:

Height of the Aquarium sheet	Thickness of the
Up to 12 inches	1/4 inch
12 to 18 inches	3/8 inch
18 to 24 inches	1/2 inch
24 to 30 inches	3/4 inch

Other Essential Items:

Two Silicone Tubes: You need to buy two tubes of good quality silicone sealants. Having two big tubes is a good idea as you may use the second silicone tube if the first one runs out while you are halfway through the task of aquarium making. You can go in for the regular household silicone. GE silicone 1 is another better option.

Painters tape or electrical tape is also required.

A caulking gun if the silicone tubes are big.

A right angle to make sure that the aquarium is square.

A few large containers or heavy objects for holding up the glass

Glass cutter is an optional requirement.

Sand paper is also optional as you may need to sand down the edges of the glass.

You need to clean the glass pieces with acetone or other cleaning substance. After you have carefully readied the glass pieces for bottom, front, rear and two sides, you need to place down the bottom pane first on the smooth and level flooring so that the glass doesn't break.

Then cut 8 to 10 inches long strips of painters or electrical tape. You may require three or four strips of tape on each side so that the left, right, and center of each pane is firmly supported. Stick half of the each strip beneath the bottom glass and the half of the strip has to lie freely outwardly. These free flowing strips of tape will be used to support the rear, front and sides pieces of glasses.

Suppose you want a 36 inches long, 28 inches wide and 12 inches high aquarium, you need to have the glass for sides to be 27.5 inches wide as it has to fit between the 36 inches long front and rear glass. Now arrange all the glass pieces carefully.

Start with the bottom piece of the glass first by putting it down. Now add silicone to the edges of the bottom glass so that the other pieces stick to it. Now take the front or rear piece of glass and carefully keep it on the straight silicone beading and provide temporary support to it with the painters or electrical tape.

Take one of the glasses prepared for sides and firmly place it on the side of the bottom glass in a way that it gets firmly attached to the front piece of glass. Support the side piece also with the tape lying beneath the bottom glass. Once the front and side glasses are firm enough to stand on their own, check the properly with a right angle that the glasses are square.

Repeat the same process for fixing the rear glass and the glass kept for the other side.

When all the four glasses firm enough to stand on their own with the bottom glass beneath them, you have to fill the edges of all the glasses inside with the beading of silicone so that there is no chance of leakage in future. Once it is done, keep it as it is for about 48 hours after which the aquarium has to be properly checked that it is not only strong enough but also without any leaking corners.

The last step is to add water to it and see that it stays inside the aquarium. This is how you can make aquarium with your own hands and can save a lot of money.

How and Where to Install the Aquarium:

You must also consider the place where you will install the aquarium. You cannot place it just anywhere as per your whim. It is to be kept at a place where you can constantly keep an eye on it though it has to be a safe place so that the aquarium remains secure. You must select a place from where you can not only enjoy the movement of the fish but also maintain it regularly. It must be away from a place that is always busy. You must also keep the aquarium away from direct sun light so that the temperature remains stable and there is not any unwanted growth in or out of the aquarium due to the change in temperature.

Strength of the Floor to retain Weight:

Though the flooring for the aquarium seems to be a not so serious an issue, it must be considered earnestly. You must consult the expert about the flooring of the aquarium so that there is no problem in future due to flooring. The flooring has to be strong and stiff enough to withstand the weight of the aquarium. It becomes all the more important considering the large size of the aquarium.

Distance of the Electrical Outlet from Acquarium:

The electrical outlet has to be quite near to the aquarium so that the cord or wire doesn't get in the way of someone who is moving about the room. You need to be quite cautious while making arrangements of the electrical supply.

Water Supply has to be at hand:

As the water of the aquarium needs to be changed at regular intervals, the water supply has to be in quite near to the aquarium.

You need to keep in mind the points described above in detail while owning an aquarium. They will help you choose the best suitable aquarium for your home.

Creating a Comfortable Living Environment

Recommendations for filling the aquarium (soil, algae, decor elements, lighting equipment):

After you have arranged all the required equipments and accessories, you have to assemble all the equipments with utmost care and precision. You have to be quite careful about the location of the aquarium. It is to be installed at a place that is firm enough to withstand the weight of the tank filled with water. Uneven and slanted floors can damage the aquarium at any stage.

Location of the Aquarium:

While choosing the location for your aquarium, you must keep in mind a number of points. The aquarium needs to be kept away from the sources of noise and din. It has to be at a good distance from washing machines, TV sets, radios and fridges. Noise can cause nervousness and stress in the fish which will have an adverse effect on their overall well being.

Avoid keeping the aquarium close to such items as affect the temperature of the water like fires, room heaters and radiators. Most varieties of fish need to be placed at a certain temperature. The variation in the temperature of the water can make them ill and it can even be fatal.

Make sure that the aquarium is not installed near windows and doors as the strong natural light from the sun and outside can have an adverse effect on algae and fish in the aquarium. A bit of sunlight is certainly good for the well being of the fish but too strong light is not at all conducive to the growth of fish.

The Process of Filling the Gravel:

Having chosen the location for the aquarium, you need to start with the process of setting up the tank. You have to begin with the task of cleaning the gravel. Take a clean bucket and pour the gravel into it. This is an important task and if you forget to cleanse the gravel properly, you will have dirty or turbid water that will have a negative effect on the health of the fish.

After putting the gravel in the bucket, pour water on it and start washing the gravel vigorously with your hands so that the dust particles and other contaminants get removed from the gravel. After cleaning the gravel for 4 to 5 minutes, throw out the dirty water.

Repeat this process till you get totally clean gravel and clear waste water. Add the gravel, stones, rocks, artificial plants and ornaments after washing them thoroughly.

Laying the Substrate in Aquarium:

The next step is to place the gravel with caution at the bottom of the aquarium. Before you prepare the substrate, you to make sure that the aquarium is properly cleaned. With the help of a ladle or scoop, you can place the gravel. Almost half an inch thick layer of gravel is recommended. You have to make it smooth and even with your own hands. Add water gently with a saucer so that the substrate remains intact and smooth.

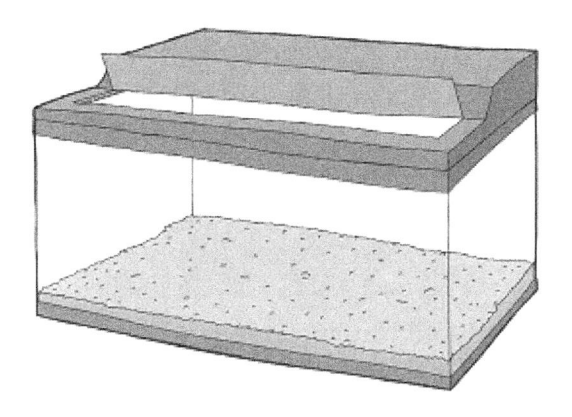

Heaters and Lights for Aquarium:

If you are going to have freshwater tropical aquarium, you need to install a heater for keeping the water warm at the right temperature. If you own a small aquarium, one heater will do but if your aquarium is large, two heaters are needed. Submersible heaters that fit inside the aquarium can be a good choice. You will do better by installing high wattage heaters as they are power efficient.

The heater has to be stable and well positioned in the aquarium. It is to be kept at a place where there is good water flow.

Temperature is to be maintained between 74 and 82 degree Fahrenheit as per the requirement of the fish species. Turn on the heater when it is immersed in water or else the heating coil or element can overheat and can get damaged in the water. Check the temperature for about 24 hours before you put fish into the aquarium.

There has to be a proper arrangement of lights on or above the aquarium. Lighting is essential for proper growth of plants. You need to turn on lights at regular intervals at least after every 8 hours. A good quality timer comes in handy to ensure that the lights are switched on at regular intervals.

Cleaning the Filters:

Filters are really important as they help to maintain a healthy and clean water in aquarium. Filters need to be cleaned properly with water before they are used. They contain dust particles, germs, bacteria and viruses as they are stored in a warehouse for a number of days before being sold.

Decorative Elements:

Market is full of innumerable decor elements exclusively designed to beautify aquariums. You can choose the ones that you like. Natural stones, ornaments, artificial plants, real plants, tree roots and gravel greatly enhance the beauty of your aquarium. All these decor elements must be washed with warm water before being placed inside the aquarium. Make sure that you buy these decorative elements from some reliable aquatic shop. Avoid using the stones and plants from your own garden as they may be harmful for the fish.

It is recommended to use both real and artificial plants in aquarium. Artificial plants add to the beauty of the tank and real plants help maintain the quality of water by absorbing surplus nitrates. There is a wide variety of artificial plants made of plastic, carbon fiber and silk that are easily available at any good aquatic shop.

Make sure that you have added electrical equipments to the aquarium before placing the plants in it. The aquarium should be filled with 50% of the total water when the plants are being kept in it. This will avoid damage to the plants.

Description of How to Control Water Parameters at Initial Stages:

The different fish species have a different requirement of water as they have acclimatized themselves to specific conditions and water temperatures. The factors like hardness of water, acidity content (pH) and oxygen level determine the living conditions for fish. The aquarium too is a water world and you have to keep in mind the different needs of different fish species.

pH Content in Aquarium Water:

The pH content in water indicates the level of hydrogen ions in aquarium water. It tells how acidic the water is. The lower level of pH stands for more acidity in water. The pH of one means the water is extremely acidic. The pH of 14 is very alkaline and pH 7 stands for neutral water conditions.

As a beginner the pH level in your aquarium has to between 6.5 and 7.5. You can test the pH level of aquarium water with the help of easy to use commercial test kits that are easily available at good aquarium supply stores. The pH content is affected by such factors as the level of fish waste and carbon dioxide. You should the pH level of your aquarium almost every week for ensuring good water quality. Any sudden drop in the pH content indicates an increase in carbon dioxide and toxic ammonia. Partial replacement of water can be done to resolve this issue.

Hardness of Water: The amount of minerals such as magnesium and calcium determine the hardness of water. The more the content, the harder the water is. The hardness of water is judged from hardness scale also known as dH. In the hardness scale, the water ranging from 4 to 8 degrees is said to be soft and water ranging between 18 and 30 degrees is hard. Most freshwater fish live comfortable in water ranging between 3 and 14 degrees of hardness. Commercial test kits to check and change the water hardness are available with fish suppliers.

Thermometer:

In order to check the water temperature in your aquarium, you need to have good quality and accurate thermometer. There are two types of thermometers available in the market i.e. the internal thermometer and the external thermometers. The internal thermometers are either fixed or float in the water and the external ones are normally stuck-on types. The internal thermometers are more accurate, whereas the external ones give lower readings by a couple of degrees.

It is recommended that you should have two thermometers to observe your aquarium temperature closely and ascertain the accuracy of each unit.

Proper Aeration:

Fish need a high level of oxygen to survive in water. In aquarium filter does the job of aeration by circulating water. You can also install an external air pump to move air through one or more air stones in the aquarium. The air pump increases oxygen level and water circulation. They help to remove carbon dioxide, toxic ammonia and carbon monoxide. The good circulation helps to maintain uniform water temperature in the aquarium.

Air Pumps for Aquarium:

There are two types of air pumps i.e. the diaphragm type and the piston type. The former is much easier to use and are also maintenance free for the beginners in aquarium keeping. The piston pumps are more powerful and suitable for larger aquariums. Consult your local aquarium retailer to procure suitable air pump for your aquarium.

Aquarium Air stones:

Made up of porous rock, an air stone allows air to cross through it. The air stone further splits the airstream into small bubbles. The bubbles slowly move to the surface and stir the water. You can easily get specially designed air stones at any aquarium supply shop.

Air Hose:

Air pump and air stones need an air hose to connect the two. This flexible pipe is used to transfer air from air pump to air stone. It should by tightly attached so that the air does not get leaked at any point. Leakage of air can damage the pump and affects the efficiency of the filter. You need to buy a good quality air hose specially manufactured to be used for aquarium.

Filtering the Aquarium Water:

You need to create natural water conditions in the aquarium so that the fish species get suitable living conditions. In the natural environment, the process of filtering occurs naturally and the toxic substances, fish wastes and other harmful contents get removed naturally. Whereas in the closed aquariums, fish need to be provided perfect living conditions. The filter in aquarium serves the purpose of removing toxic substances.

There are three types of filtration systems i.e. mechanical, chemical, and biological. Mechanical filters physically eliminate suspended particles from the water by passing it through a fine filter medium. External power filters and canister filters provide rapid mechanical filtration. Chemical filters chemically treat water to remove toxic substances such as fish wastes and toxic ammonia. When you fix activated carbon to an external power filter, you are providing chemical filtration. Biological filters make use of the nitrogen cycle to remove toxic compounds from the water.

A perfect example of a biological filter is the under gravel filter that draws water through the aquarium gravel. This substrate contains the necessary bacteria to change nitrogenous wastes to nitrate. Although this type of filtration requires a bit more time to establish a working bacteria colony, it provides the best kind of filtration.

Most of the commercially manufactured aquarium filters provide all three kinds of filtration. For instance, the external power filter mechanically removes particles and contaminants. It chemically removes toxins if it contains activated carbon and biologically turns nitrogenous wastes through the nitrogen cycle in its filter media. Some types of filters available to the beginner include the internal box filter, the external power filter, the external canister filter, and the under gravel filter. These are certainly not the only types of filters available, but they are the most common.

Choosing the right filter for your new aquarium can be a bit confusing, considering the different kinds. We have tried to facilitate the task by giving a short description of the each type with its major pros and cons.

Internal Box Filter:

The internal box filter is attached inside the water tank. An external air pump is used to push air forcefully into the aquarium. Layers of filter media treat water mechanically, chemically and also biologically.

Driven by air, this filter is effective at the aeration and circulation of the water. The box filter does not provide adequate levels of filtration for the aquarium above 20 gallons. This filter is simply too small to treat the fish waste and debris that accumulate in the aquarium. It also needs frequent cleaning,

External Power Filter:

The external power filter is the least complicated and simplest filter system for a beginner in fish keeping. These filters purify water using all three kinds of filtering systems. They are specifically designed to run large aquariums. The external power filter is attached on the outer side of the aquarium. It too has its own motor to supply power. A u-shaped flexible hose is used to put water into the filter from where it percolates through layers of fibrous material. The water too passes through activated carbon and sent back to the aquarium by means of a pipe. The power filter provides circulation and aeration to the water. This filter is quite effective at removing debris and fish waste from the tank. It does not require much cleaning like other filters do. Moreover, cleaning these filters is an easy task.

External Canister Filter:

External canister filters are more advanced filters. Much larger than others, this filter is designed to be used in large aquariums above 50 gallons. The canister filter is made up of a large canister that is normally attached close to the aquarium. Like other filters, this filter has filter media and activated carbon. It has a powerful motor to filter huge amounts of water. Water is drawn up by a suction pipe and sent back to the aquarium by means of a well positioned pipe.

Under gravel Filter:

Effective at providing the best results in biological filtering system, the under gravel filter comprises a plastic plate that is attached under the substrate of the aquarium. An external air pump is used to force water through gravel to the underlying filter. These filters are really good at providing aeration and water circulation.

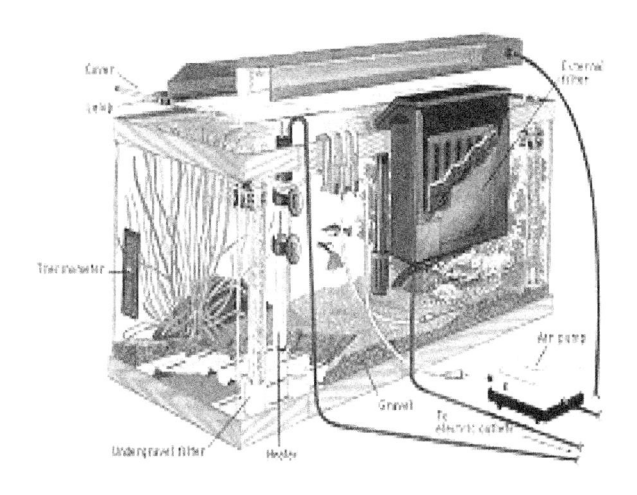

The Nitrogen Cycle:

Fish are living organisms that need oxygen to burn energy obtained from food. The fish waste gets accumulated in the water in the form of carbon dioxide and toxic ammonia. These wastes must be removed to keep the fish healthy. Carbon dioxide normally gets eliminated from water through aeration at the surface. Photosynthesis too helps in the removal of carbon dioxide. Nitrogen cycle converts toxic substances into less toxic substances.

In nature, the nitrogen cycle converts toxic substances such as ammonia and wastes into harmless products by bacterial colonies. There is a specific species of bacteria that converts fish wastes into ammonia, ammonia into nitrite, and nitrite gets converted into nitrate. Thereafter nitrate is used by plants as a fertilizer and subsequently gets removed from the water. A balanced nitrogen cycle is conducive to the good health and well being of an aquarium.

The Process of Launching Fish into the Aquarium:

Fill up the tank with a flexible pipe. You can use tap too if there is one at hand or else you should use a bucket to fill water. Having filled the aquarium with water, add high quality water de-chlorinator to it. Avoid using chlorine as it is not good for fish.

If you have decided to use live plants, you have to plant the roots tenderly beneath the surface of the substrate. Make arrangements for keeping the plants moist till they are planted. Proper lighting is required for the growth of plants.

Fill your tank with water just a couple of inches below the topmost point so that there is some space for air between the water and the hood.

While introducing fish to the new aquarium, you have to be patient and cautious. It is not advisable to fill the tank with different fish breeds in a hurried and haphazard manner. You need to put 2 or 3 fish every second week to the aquarium and monitor closely the movement of the fish.

Choose hardy fish species and also select a few algae controlling species such as Ancistrus and Pencil Fish. These algae controlling species are required only if your aquarium has real plants in it. Fish that consume algae will control the excessive growth of algae in the initial stages and when the plants are established, they will help control the growth of algae.

While stocking the aquarium, you have to select healthy fish. The symptoms of healthy fish are being enlisted here.

Healthy fish have clear eyes and undamaged fins. Their scales are intact and parallel to their bodies. Healthy fish do not have bloated stomachs and there are no white spots on the body or fins.

They are active with steady respiration rate. Gills are not faded and discoloured.

Make sure that no sick fish gets inside your aquarium. You can take the help from some professional aquarist while selecting the fish for your aquarium. Selecting healthy fish in the beginning will save you from unnecessary problems subsequently. You can maintain a small quarantine tank for the observation of newly purchased fish. This quarantine tank is like a clinic where the sick fish is kept under observation. After observing the movement and activities of fish for a week or two, you can shift it to the regular aquarium.

Switch off the lights of aquarium during acclimatization period. Float the bag containing the fish in the aquarium for about 20 minutes so that the new fish gets adapted to the new temperature. Open the bag and gently pour about some water from aquarium into it. Let the bag remain in this condition for next 10 minutes. Repeat this process for two more times after every 10 minutes. Hereafter open the bag and gently place the fish in the aquarium. Carefully observe their movement for next 24 hours before feeding them.

Proper Care for Fish

Description of additives for water and vitamin complexes necessary for different types of fish and different types of water:

Fish in your aquarium need to feel as much at home as in the natural environment. You must make arrangements to protect the aquarium fish and transform their world into biotope-like water. Clean aquarium water and optimal water quality need to be ensured. Best quality water additives need to be used while setting up a new aquarium and during partial water change. To ensure the well being of fish, they need to be used at different stages. Tap water normally contains heavy metals like zinc, lead and copper. To make the water suitable to the requirements of the fish, it must be clean and devoid of bacteria, viruses, heavy metals, contaminants, chlorine and chloramine. The water is made suitable for fish by neutralising these substances by making use of high quality water conditioners.

Essential Vitamins for Your Fish:

Fish need to be given vitamins for good health just like any other animal. An incomplete diet can give rise to vitamin and nutrient deficiencies. It can further lead to a number of problems such as the onset of serious conditions like stunted growth, weak immune system and also death. Vitamin supplements, along with a nutritious diet, are the best way to keep your fish healthy and happy.

Vitamin A: Crustaceans and greens are the rich sources of this essential vitamin. Essential for normal growth and physical development. It is also important for proper formation of scales and bones.

Vitamin B Complex: Greens and fish eggs are good sources of this vitamin. It has a number of health benefits such as good digestion, proper growth, proper functioning of the nervous system, digestion of nutrients, and well being of the slime coat.

Vitamin C: The major sources of this essential nutrient are algae, greens and fish eggs. It is important for the prevention of diseases. It helps in the proper digestion, quick healing and proper formation and working of skeleton. It also imparts glowing coating to the skin.

Vitamin D: Snails, earthworms and shrimps are major sources of vitamin D. It is required for phosphorous and calcium metabolization which leads to the development of scales and bones.

Vitamin K : Another important nutrient, vitamin K is derived from greens, water fleas and liver. It helps in blood coagulation.

Recommendations for Monitoring the Life of Aquarium:

After you have introduced the fish to the aquarium, you have to be quite careful about their movements. You have to monitor their activities closely and maintain their new home in accordance with the requirement of the fish species. Now you have to feed the fish, closely observe them and look after the cleanliness of water and aquarium. Acquaint yourself with the fish and be competent enough to understand their behaviour. Be particular about the signs of diseases if any. Closely observe the live plants and if you find any dead parts, remove them at once so that the water remains healthy. Make sure that the aquarium is stable in all respects, be it temperature, water quality and health of fish. The water temperature has to be stable and uniform without any fluctuation. Examine the heater, the filter, lights, air pump and air stones on a regular basis to make sure that they are in perfect working condition. You have to devote a few minutes of your day-to-day life to ensure the well being of your fish.

Cleanliness of the Aquarium:

Cleanliness of the aquarium is an essential requirement. You have to be an active and disciplined caretaker of your fish. Indifference and negligence on your part will ultimately lead to the poor water quality with the passage of time. Make sure that you are committed enough to the task of aquarium keeping.

Vacuuming of the Aquarium: Vacuuming is of utmost importance to ensure the cleanliness of aquarium. With the lapse of time, detritus may accumulate in the substrate. Detritus is a toxic substance that is a mixture of the parts of plants, uneaten food particles and fish wastes. These substances turn into toxic ammonia if not removed timely and result in the contamination of water. It eventually disturbs the balance of the aquarium. The toxic ammonia too clogs filter. Considering all these undesirable situations, vacuuming becomes all the more important. Vacuums and gravel cleaners are available with the aquarist shops.

Maintenance of the Filters:

It is very important to maintain cleanliness of the filters in the aquarium. The filters get clogged with food particles, pieces of plants and other debris. The top-level filter gets dirty easily as this collects the bigger pieces of debris. The performance of the filter gets adversely affected with the passage of time if left untreated.

Controlling Algae:

Algae are simple photosynthetic organisms that range in size from the one-celled microscopic types to big seaweeds that grow over 230 feet. Algae can manage to enter aquarium through air. They can be found in an aquarium on the surface of the water, on rocks, gravel and plants. If they are at a low level, algae can improve the overall well being of the life in your aquarium. They turn carbon dioxide into oxygen as they are photosynthetic. They also serve as food for herbivorous fish.

However excessive algae growth can be suffocating for fish. Avoiding excessive growth of algae is a must for the health and well being of fish. Sunlight and high nitrate levels are conducive to the growth of algae. You must ensure that the algae growth remains stable in the aquarium.

Healthy plants keep in check the excessive growth of algae as nitrates are consumed by the plants rather than by algae.

There are some algae eating varieties of fish such as Black Mollies, Corydoras Catfish and Flying Foxes. Stocking them in aquarium controls the excessive growth of algae.

Reducing the period of lighting by two hours from 12 to 10 hours per day.

Timely water change as per the recommended schedule contains the growth of algae.

Use an algae scraper from time to time to scrape algae from the walls of the aquarium.

Make sure that the plants, rocks, gravel and other decor elements free from algae before being placed in the aquarium.

Don't remove all the algae from the water tank. Some algae is good for the well being of fish.

Test the Water of Aquarium From Time to Time:

It is extremely important to check the quality of water from time to time for the over all well being of the aquarium and fish species. In the beginning, water needs to be tested every second day. The properties of the water in aquarium change quickly as fish are added to water in it. If water is not closely monitored, the life of the fish is threatened. After the close examination of the water for 3 or 4 weeks in the beginning, you need to test the water once a week for about next two months. After two months, the water will become stable and well established. Now you need not supervise the water every week and you can test the water once in a month. However, you need to be careful enough to notice any sudden change in the behaviour of fish. Cloudy water, excessive growth of algae, fish sickness require the test of water immediately. Water needs to be replaced at the earliest if water quality becomes poor.

Partial Replacement of Water:

It is highly recommended to change the water partially at regular intervals to keep your fish healthy. You need to remove about 10 to 20% of water every week and fill fresh and clean water in its place. Replacement of water helps maintain the quality of water. Toxic ammonia, nitrates, nitrites and other harmful substances get removed each time you replace the water. The recommended time to go in for the partial water change is when you are vacuuming your aquarium. You can also use a hose or a bucket to replace water.

Recommendations for Monitoring the Life of Fish and Feeding them :

In the aquarium, you have to look after your fish. The responsibility of feeding the fish falls on you. They

do not have to work hard to get food as fish have to do in their natural habitat. You have to provide nutritious and well-balanced diet that keeps them healthy and alive.

You need to follow a regular feeding schedule to keep the fish healthy. Food with essential nutrients, minerals, proteins and vitamins is a must for the overall well being of the fish in your aquarium. Nutritious food will keep the fish hale and hearty.

Fish can be categorized into three types on the basis of their eating habits. They are either herbivorous or omnivorous or carnivorous.

Carnivorous fish need to be fed upon dead food, live worms, pieces of shrimp and other meats in the aquarium. In their natural habitat, they feed on other smaller fish which they bite, crush or swallow.

Herbivores eat only vegetable matter such as leafy greens plants and algae. They too eat flake foods. Their diet can be supplemented with some household vegetables such as green beans, pieces cauliflower and peas. An excellent example of the herbivorous fish is the Angelfish.

Omnivorous fish species eat flakes, live foods, and bits of table food. They will eat almost anything. As they are clearly the easiest fish to feed, they are highly recommended for beginners in aquarium keeping. You must offer them a variety of food to meet their dietary requirements.

There are a number of high quality products in the market for feeding fish. You can consult books and professional pet store staff about the food to be fed to the fish.

You must know the feeding requirements of fish species, both herbivorous and omnivorous, in your aquarium.

There is a wide variety of foods for aquarium fish. Natural foods include fresh, frozen and dried items. Leafy greens, green vegetables and fish or invertebrate flesh are some famous natural fish foods.

There are also prepared foods that are commercially sold for aquarium fish. The flakes, pellets, tablets, crumbs and dry foods are some of the famous prepared foods. Prepared foods are available in different forms in accordance with the requirements of different fish species. Large fish are given pellets instead of flakes as they eat a large morsel. The fish lying at the bottom are also fed pellets rather than flakes as flakes usually float on the surface of water.

Live food is a major source of nutrition to the aquarium fish. They impart rich colors and good growth to the fish. The common live foods are earthworms, black worms, feeder fish, bloodworms and brine shrimp.

How to Feed the Fish in Your Aquarium:

The most common problem faced by beginners in aquarium keeping is related to how much food is to be fed to the fish and how often it is to be offered.

Some fish species are gluttons and some are not very eager eaters. Many of the experts say that feeding little is much better than feeding too much. You can follow the guidelines enlisted below to feed your fish:

Offer as much food as your fish will eat in about five or six minutes. Provide pellets and tablets to the fish at bottom. Flakes should be given to the fish lying on the surface and in the middle of the aquarium.

Never feed the fish too much though you might feel the fish need more food. Overeating will have a negative effect on your fish. It will be stressed and lazy. Uneaten food will turn into a toxic substance in the water of the tank which will degrade water quality.

If you are at home during day time, feed your fish from time to time by offering small pieces of food. If you are not away from home during the day, make it a routine to feed your fish twice a day at the same time day every day. Feed the fish once in the morning and secondly at night.

Make it a point to feed your fish at the same place in the aquarium.

Observe all your aquarium fish closely during feeding and make sure that each of the fish gets enough food. Do not forget that different fish species are to be fed at different levels in the aquarium. Some fish do not go to the surface to eat and wait for the food to reach the water level where they stay. Pellets and tablets that go down to the bottom should be provided for the

fish living there. Keep in mind that the refusal to eat is one of the first symptoms of illness. Notice the movement of the fish and be watchful about any abnormal behaviour by fish. Feed the fish about half an hour after turning on the light.

Make use of dry and frozen foods to avoid chances of the transmission of disease. Keep dry food away from moisture and also avoid using wet hands to feed the fish. Also avoid feeding live fish to large predatory fish species.

If you are going to be away from your aquarium for an extended period, make arrangements

for someone to feed your fish. You can also install an automatic food dispenser. If you use the food dispenser to feed fish, make sure that there has to be long intervals between feeding times.

These are some common rules that you can follow to feed your fish. You can also consult your local aquarium dealer or a veterinarian who can help you with the task of feeding your fish.

Maintenance of the Aquarium:

- You need to follow the schedule given below to maintain the aquarium:
- Tasks to be Done on Daily Basis:
- You have to give food to fish twice a day.
- Keeping an eye on the water temperature.
- Lights to be turned on and off.
- Make sure that the heaters are in perfect working condition.
- Check the filter daily and be particular about its proper functioning.
- Aerator too needs to be checked daily.

Tasks to be Performed Weekly:

- Observe the fish minutely and make sure that they are healthy. Make a note of the signs of diseases.
- Vacuum the aquarium every week.
- Exchange as much as 10 % water. Make sure that you add clean water to the aquarium.

- Weekly test of the water for nitrates, pH and level of minerals.
- Examine the filter and check if the top mat needs to be changed.
- Prune the water plants and fertilize them on the weekly basis.

Works to be Done after a Month:

- Scrape the insides of the aquarium to maintain the level of algae.
- Test of the water for nitrates, pH and level of minerals.
- Vacuum the aquarium properly and remove toxic ammonia to keep water clean.
- Rinse the plants, rocks and stones to remove algae and detritus.
- Trim the real plants. Add fertilizers to keep them healthy.

Tasks to be Done on Quarterly Basis:

- Make sure that you replace the old water strictly in accordance with your routine.
- Test of the water for nitrates, pH and level of minerals.
- Vacuum the aquarium properly and remove toxic ammonia to keep water clean.
- Rinse the plants, rocks and stones to remove algae and detritus. Do replace some of them if needed.
- Trim the real plants. Add fertilizers to keep them healthy.
- Replace the air stones.

Maintenance of Aquarium after a Year:

- Restart the aquarium all over again.
- Wash all the gravel, stones. rocks and artificial plants.
- Replace the air stones.
- Remove filter to make sure that it is in good working condition. Replace at least 50% of the media with a new mat and charcoal.
- Empty the aquarium. Just leave some original water to help condition the aquarium.

Health of the Fish in Aquarium:

You must ensure the good health of fish in your aquarium. Fish are prone to a number of diseases if kept in unhealthy conditions. Harmful bacteria, viruses and parasites can enter the aquarium any time and cause serious diseases. These pathogens can also enter with new fish and water. Many of the fish diseases are highly contagious and can even be fatal. The task to keep your fish healthy is not so difficult if you remain a bit careful. You need to recognize the symptoms of diseases and you can easily do this with a bit of effort.

Description of Symptoms and Diseases of the Fish and Cures:

You must be capable enough to recognize the signs of ailments in your aquarium. The appearance and behaviour of the fish can tell you about the sickness. You must closely examine the behaviour and movement of the fish on a regular basis to be acquainted with the symptoms of diseases.

If any of the fish show slow movement and erratic behaviour, it is not a good sign. Improper eating routine, lack of appetite too are matters of concern. Rubbing the body against the walls and objects in the aquarium, unnatural behaviour, bloated stomach, cloudy eyes, twitching fins and hyperventilation of the gills are some other signs of the diseases.

If you are a beginner in aquarium keeping, you need to go in for the commercial treatment by professional aquarists rather than opting for home based remedies. It is recommended to consult your fish supplier if the fish in your aquarium are unwell. Consulting a veterinarian is also a good idea to treat fish. Be particular about the instructions given by the medical expert and follow the directions in letter and spirit.

Common Ailments affecting Fish:

There are innumerable diseases affect fish. Some of these diseases get transferred between different species and some are related to some particular fish species. Some of these ailments are contagious and some are not. The fish in the aquarium suffer from a number of diseases and the most common of them are being enlisted below with their cures.

Indigestion: A fish suffering from poor digestion or constipation remain inactive and lazy. Usually they lie at the bottom of the tank. They may have bloated stomach. This issue may have something to do with the poor quality of food or may be due to the food that does not get along some particular fish species.

Cure: You should at once stop feeding the food that is being given to the ill fish. Take the fish away from regular aquarium and keep in in the hospital tank for a few days to monitor its movement. Make sure you give it the food that is compatible with that species. Place the fish back in the aquarium once it starts behaving normally. It is a common problem that you may face over and over again.

Swim Bladder Disease: This disease is quite easy to deal with. The affected fish cannot swim properly as it might be suffering from loss of balance due to bruising of the swim bladder due to fighting, constipation, and bacterial infection caused by poor water quality.

Cure: As the wound heals, the fish becomes normal. Make sure that the water quality is good. Changing the food or diet of the fish can also help you overcome this problem.

Pinecone Disease: Also known as kidney bloat because the stomach bloats to such an extent that it becomes easily noticeable. The scales come out like a pinecone. The poor quality of the water is one of the reasons for this disease and normally fish do not survive once they get afflicted with this disease.

It is normally believed that this disease is not curable. It is recommended to isolate the fish and if the fish does not recover, it is advisable to kill it painlessly.

Tumours: If you notice any unnatural growth like lumps, large blisters or warts on the body of fish, you must consult the veterinarian and get the tumour surgically excised.

Exophthalmus: Also known as pop-eye, this disease can be identified by observing the bulging eyes of fish. The poor water quality is normally responsible for this ailment that can be cured by improving the water quality.

Cure: Make sure that the water quality remains up to the mark.

There are many diseases that are caused by fungal, viral or bacterial infection. Most of these diseases are contagious.

Furunculosis: A contagious disease, furunculosis is a bacterial infection that spreads at a fast pace. The flesh beneath the scales get affected. Bleeding ulcers appear under the scales.

Cure: There is a definite cure of this ailment. The survival rate is quite low and experts recommend that the fish suffering from this ulcer disease should be humanely destroyed.

Ulcers: Ulcers start as an infection and develop into big ulcers and warts. They appear under fins in the form of red ulcers. They do not swell and gradually eat away into the body.

Cure: The affected fish is to be isolated soon after this disease is identified. The medicated food and antibiotics need to be fed strictly in accordance with the instructions by a veterinarian.

Body Slime Fungus: This disease is highly contagious and can kill your fish within two days if you are not able to recognize the symptoms. The mucous coating of the fish starts to come off, and the body turns red.

Cure: Isolate the affected fish in the hospital tank. Contact your veterinarian immediately. Remedy is to be administered quickly.

Mouth Fungus Disease. A bacterial disease, it first appears in the form of white growth on the mouth. It also affects the fins, gills and back. This disease can be fatal if left untreated for long.

Cure: Isolate the fish as early as possible and give the salt bath to the affected fish in the hospital tank. Its cures are available in the form of bacterial control agents. Do consult the professional aquarist to deal with this disease.

Fish Pox: Specific to some species like goldfish, carp and koi, this is a viral disease that first appears in the form of white or gray coating on the skin of fish.

Cure: This is not a contagious disease. However you need to take precautionary measures and isolate the afflicted fish for about 7 or 8 days and that much time is sufficient for this ailment to disappear.

China Disease: One of the deadliest disease that is bound to kill the fish finally. Its symptoms are the discolouration of the fins. The affected areas become black gradually.

Cure: There is no cure for this highly contagious disease. The affected fish should be killed painlessly and other fish in the aquarium must be put in the hospital tank for salt water treatment.

Fin Rot: Another contagious disease that is caused by fighting among fish and poor water quality. It is easily noticeable as the fins lose their parts. Sometimes the entire fin get eaten away gradually.

Cure: Consult your veterinarian for the remedy and make arrangements to treat the water as this contagious disease may affect other fish too.

There are some other parasitic diseases caused by fish lice, anchor worm, leeches and flukes.

Recommendations on Drugs and Treatment:

The traditional Salt Bath: This is a tried and tested treatment given to fish suffering from a number of diseases like the itch, fin rot and fungus. The hospital tank is used mainly for saltwater bath. This treatment requires adding a teaspoon of table salt for one gallon of water in the hospital tank. This treatment is done for about 7 or 8 days with the saltwater bath being done usually twice a day.

Emergent Washing and Cleaning of Aquarium: If you find the above mentioned diseases affecting 3 or 4 fish, you must perform an immediate cleaning of the aquarium. Make arrangements to place your fish in the hospital tank when the aquarium is being cleaned. You have to start everything all over again. Remove filter media and take out the contents of the aquarium. Wash the walls, rocks, gravel, artificial plants and filter with high quality bleach. You need to throw out the contents to avoid any chances of the spread of infection. Take out the heater and wash it with bleach. You need to replace most of the contents and properly wash electrical appliances.

Measures for Disease Prevention:

You have to be extra cautious and watchful for the timely prevention of diseases. Daily inspection and observation of the aquarium can be an effective measure to prevent the chances of the spread of diseases. There can be other issues which can later on turn into serious problems. If you notice fish with damaged or injured body parts, it may be the sign of fighting. Timely diagnosis and treatment of the problems will save you from unnecessary trouble later on.

As a disease can affect any living organism at any point of time, fish stocked in the aquarium too can be afflicted with disease at any stage. You must take preventive measures rather than wait for the problem to arise. You'd better keep in mind the following tips for preventing disease:

Select only healthy fish by consulting an expert in this field and avoid buying sick fish.

Do not buy too many fish at a time. Purchase only a few and observe their movement for at least a week or two.

Make sure that the fish get properly acclimatized before being placed into the aquarium.

Always condition new water properly. Metals, chlorine and chloramine are harmful to the fish in acquarium.

Exercise caution while repairing and fixing the aquarium.

Maintenance of the aquarium is to be done from time to time. Water too is to be tested at regular intervals.

Make sure that the temperature in the aquarium remains stable. Temperature variation may cause serious problems for fish.

All rights Reserved. No part of this publication or the information in it may be quoted from or reproduced in any form by means such as printing, scanning, photocopying or otherwise without prior written permission of the copyright holder.

Disclaimer and Terms of Use: Effort has been made to ensure that the information in this book is accurate and complete, however, the author and the publisher do not warrant the accuracy of the information, text and graphics contained within the book due to the rapidly changing nature of science, research, known and unknown facts and internet. The Author and the publisher do not hold any responsibility for errors, omissions or contrary interpretation of the subject matter herein. This book is presented solely for motivational and informational purposes only.

Printed in Great Britain
by Amazon